# *Heart to Heart*

## ~Inspirational Poems~

A collection of original poems; written to bring laughter, joy, peace, encouragement, healing, comfort, and inspiration.

**Dr. Irma S. White**

Copyright © 2007 by Dr. Irma S. White

*Heart to Heart*
*Inspirational Poems*
by Dr. Irma S. White

Printed in the United States of America

ISBN 978-1-60266-471-5

All rights reserved solely by the author. The author guarantees all contents are original and do not infringe upon the legal rights of any other person or work. No part of this book may be reproduced in any form without the permission of the author. The views expressed in this book are not necessarily those of the publisher.

Unless otherwise indicated, Bible quotations are taken from *The Holy Bible, New International Version, and the Full Life Study Bible*. Copyright © 1992 by Life Publishers International. Used by permission of Zondervan Publishing House.

www.xulonpress.com

# Dedication

This book of original poems is dedicated to my mother, Wardell Hall Simmons, born January 28, 1919, to the late Annie and Robert Hall. She moved from this temporary earthly home April 11, 2005. Wardell was a strong, brave, and virtuous woman of God who always enjoyed the simple pleasures of life, family, friends, church, and home. Her smiles were precious and worth viewing, and her laughter brought warmth to the hearts who heard it.

# Table of Contents

Dedication ..................................................... v
Acknowledgments ........................................ xv
Comments about the Poems ........................ xvii
Introduction ................................................. xix

**Chapter I: Comfort**
Isaiah 49:13: *"For the Lord comforts his people."*

A Heavenly Perspective .............................. 23
Comfort ....................................................... 24
Fallen Soldier .............................................. 25
Jesus Is Here ............................................... 26
Jesus Is the Answer .................................... 28
Jesus, You're Always the Same .................. 30
Just Ask ...................................................... 31
Letters from Heaven ................................... 32
Happy Thanksgiving from Your Family in
    Heaven ................................................. 33
Happy Thanksgiving from Your Father and
    Grandmother ....................................... 34
Happy Thanksgiving from Your Grandmother ...... 35

*Heart to Heart*

Merry Christmas ......................................................36
Praise Your Way Out...............................................37
Thank You, Father....................................................38
Thank You God, for Being God .............................39
Word Portrait of Mom.............................................40

*This is the end of the poems from heaven*

## Chapter II: Encouragement

2 Thessalonians 2:16: *"May the Lord Jesus Christ himself and God our Father, encourage your hearts."*

God Came .................................................................45
God Does Supply ......................................................47
God Is Awesome and Great......................................48
God Is........................................................................50
God Is Here ..............................................................52
God's Love................................................................53
He's in Charge..........................................................54
Honor Your Father ...................................................55
I Love You, Lord......................................................57
I'll Fight for You ......................................................58
It's a Temp Job .........................................................60
New Beginnings........................................................61
New School, First Day .............................................62
Our Special Day........................................................63
Receive Your Reward...............................................64
See Through His Eyes...............................................66
Shine Your Light ......................................................67
The Father's Love .....................................................68
We Win! ...................................................................69
Your Light Is On ......................................................70

*Heart to Heart*

You've Got to Press Through ...............................71

## Chapter III: Growth
Colossians 2:19: *"It grows as God causes it to grow."*

Fertile Ground.......................................................75
Growing Through Affirmation..............................76
Growth Through Affliction ..................................77
Handling Adversity ..............................................78
Lose Your Mind ...................................................80
Love Is .................................................................81
Valleys..................................................................82
Where Is the Child? .............................................83

## Chapter IV: Healing
Psalm 107:20: *"He sent forth his word and healed them."*

A Pat on the Back.................................................87
Be Affirmed..........................................................88
Be Whole ..............................................................89
Free Through Praise .............................................90
Is It Fair?...............................................................91
It's Okay................................................................92
Let Them Go .........................................................93
Lonely and Bound.................................................94
Radical Praise........................................................96
Set Me Free ...........................................................98
Warfare Praise .......................................................99
What Happened?....................................................100
What to Do When You Feel Alone.......................102

*Heart to Heart*

## Chapter V: Joy
Psalm 19:8: *"The precepts of the Lord are right, giving joy to the heart."*

A Daughter Like You ...........................................105
A Father's Daughter............................................106
Happy Birthday, Son...........................................107
Our Daughter, the Ambassador...........................108
Sow Joy................................................................110
Special Thoughts of You ....................................112
Tanya's Special Day............................................113

## Chapter VI: Laughter
Psalm 126: *"Our mouths were filled with laughter."*

Growing Old .......................................................117
Growth ................................................................118
Laughter ..............................................................119
Maturing..............................................................121
Our Sister, the Speller ........................................122
Signs of Maturing ..............................................123

## Chapter VII: Peace
Micah 5:5: *"He will be their peace."*

2 Thessalonians 3:16: *"The Lord of peace himself gives you peace at all times and in every way."*

Focus on Him.......................................................127
The Promised Seed .............................................128
The Revealed Word..............................................131
The Word..............................................................133

*Heart to Heart*

## Chapter VIII: Understanding
Colossians 2:2: *"Have the full riches of complete understanding."*

| | |
|---|---|
| A Moment in Time | 137 |
| Are You Available? | 138 |
| Are You Prepared to Receive? | 139 |
| Being | 140 |
| Best Use | 141 |
| Birthing a Seed | 142 |
| Check Your Fruit | 144 |
| Disasters! Why? | 145 |
| Do You Hear Him? | 146 |
| Fruit Inspector | 147 |
| Get the Big Picture | 148 |
| Go with the Flow | 149 |
| Know Your Assignment | 150 |
| Make It Clear | 152 |
| Obey God | 153 |
| Promised Success | 154 |
| Teach Me, O Lord | 155 |
| Understand Your Role | 157 |
| Where Is God? | 159 |
| Why Christmas? | 160 |
| Why Inspirational Poems? | 161 |
| Yielded Vessel | 163 |
| Your Journey | 164 |
| Your Life Is Not Your Own | 166 |

## Chapter IX: Why You Are Here

Luke 16:15: *"Go into all the world and preach the good news to all creation."*

Matthew 28:19-20: *"Go and make disciples of all nations, baptizing them in the name of the Father, Son and of the Holy Spirit, teaching them to obey everything I have commanded you."*

Destiny ................................................................169
Go Get Your Land ...............................................170
God Has a Plan....................................................171
God Has Need of You ..........................................172
It Is Yours, Come and Get It ...............................173
Ministry...............................................................174
Naked and Unashamed ........................................175
New Things I Declare ..........................................176
One Minute ..........................................................177
Purpose................................................................178
Read the Book......................................................179
Run in Your Lane ................................................180
Speak God's Word ...............................................181
Submit..................................................................183
Suit Up!................................................................184
Surrender..............................................................185
Task on Demand ..................................................186
Tell Me God, What's My Plan .............................187
The Battle Is On!..................................................189
The Call................................................................191
The Walk ..............................................................192
The War Is On ......................................................193
We Are Passing Through.......................................194

xii

*Heart to Heart*

We Are Sent .........................................196
What's First? .......................................197
What's for Me Today? Just Be! ...........198
What's My Part? .................................200
What's Your Lane? ..............................201

# Acknowledgments

**Family Members**

To my spouse, Dr. Zinerva White Jr., thanks for your persistent encouragement and technical assistance. Without you, this book would not be published.

To all of my daughters and sons: Janet White, Zinerva White III, Anthony White, Leah White and Tanya White, thanks for encouraging me to complete and publish this book of poems.

**Technical Assistants**

Carminisa McLean, Pastors Michael and Camela Nelson, and Sylvester Andre Poole III: thanks for taking the time to assist in providing the necessary skills to publish this book of poems.

## Proofreaders

Leah White, Kristin McCarty, Sylvester Andre Poole III, and Anna George Robinson: thanks for taking the time to proofread all the poems for this book.

# Comments About the Poems from Pastors

Your poems really ministered to us. They must be shared with others.
*Pastors Garry and Cathy Spriggs*

You must get your poems published. Others will be blessed when they read them.
*Pastors James and Francine Wright*

The poems you shared with me really ministered to me. I feel so uplifted and encouraged.
*Rev. Dr. Edith Charity*

Have you published your book of poems yet? People are waiting for them. They need to read them. They will be so blessed by them.
*Pastors Michael and Camela Nelson*

*Heart to Heart*

You are doing a great job. I can't wait to get a copy of your poem book. By you sharing your poems at our church, they ministered to so many people. Our members have been blessed by just hearing some of your poems.

*Pastors Jerry and Christal Kellam*

# Introduction

Heart to Heart is a collection of poems written to bring comfort, encouragement, growth, healing, joy, laughter, peace, and understanding. You will enjoy reading the poems in this book if you have ever wondered about any of the following things: Why are you here on earth at this time in history; why do good people die; why, after losing a loved one, is the grief still deep within you and nothing seems to comfort you? Why do you have problems forgiving an offense; why have you been in difficult situations one after another and there seems to be no relief? Why have you had problems with your memory lately; why, you have wondered, "God, where are You in the midst of my troubles?" Why did Jesus come to earth; why did God love you so much that He sent His Son to redeem you; and why have you had problems understanding the Bible? Now you can stop your wondering. Most of your concerns will be answered when you read these poems.

As you read *Heart to Heart*, think about how wonderful it is to receive answers from the heart of the Father to the heart of man. The Father takes great pleasure in answering all of your concerns. This book is a collection of original poems inspired by the Holy Spirit to bring comfort, encouragement, growth, and healing through life's experiences. The poems in this book will make you ponder over your relationship with others, your relationship with God the Father, God the Son, and God the Holy Spirit. This book will encourage you, uplift you, and inspire you mentally, physically, emotionally, and spiritually.

*Letters from Heaven* are grouped together and are not in traditional alphabetic order. They are meant to bring comfort to those who are still grieving from the lost of loved ones.

### 2 Thessalonians 2:16-17
May our Lord Jesus Christ himself and God our Father, who loved us and by his grace gave us eternal encouragement and good hope, encourage your hearts and strengthen you in every good deed and word.

# Chapter I: Comfort

Isaiah 49:13: *"For the Lord comforts his people."*

*Heart to Heart*

# A Heavenly Perspective

From a heavenly perspective we send
Greetings to you from those who have been
Dear to us and now to heaven they have gone
No longer can we reach them by telephone.

In hopes that from your sorrow and your grief
This heavenly perspective will bring you relief.
So, Happy Thanksgiving though Mom's away
Be happy, share cheer on this Thanksgiving Day.

### Revelation 19:7

"Let us rejoice and be glad and give him the glory!"

# Comfort

What can you say
When one passes away?
We know we all will go one day.
We did not come to earth to stay.

Even when we know
Just where we will go,
With the Lord forever to abide,
Still there's that pain deep down inside.

How do you soothe that kind of pain?
Even when you know you'll see them again?
The nagging pain down so deep,
That you feel even while you sleep.

Time, they say, heals all things,
And only the good memories to you brings.
Until then we must all depend,
On the God of all comfort, who dwells within.

### 2 Corinthians 1:3-4

"Praise be to the God and Father of our Lord Jesus Christ, the Father of compassion and the God of all comfort, who comforts us in all our troubles, so that we can comfort those in any trouble with the comfort we ourselves have received from God."

# Fallen Soldier

Today, I was clearly awakened.
A bit startled and very shaken
A little teary and a little sad.
Gone, a fallen soldier that I had.

A loyal soldier, a brave one, too.
Many a battle we fought through.
In the storms and in the rain,
We would fight and victory gain.

He went ahead to see how things are.
He's no longer here, but not very far.
He fought a good fight, he's won the race.
Now he's in a far better place.

There's still that pain deep inside.
Feels as if a part of me died.
Though I hurt and shed a tear,
And wish that he was still here.

I'll see him again and so will you.
We're all in a battle, fighting our way through.
A good soldier has fallen today,
The battle of faith never went away.

*2 Samuel 1:25*
"How are the mighty fallen in the midst of the battle!"

*Heart to Heart*

# Jesus Is Here

Don't you fret, doubt, or fear
Your loving Savior is always here.
When sorrow, confusion, and pain
Seem to come down like rain.

In the midst of trouble you raise
Your hands up high and give Him praise
This stops all that terrible pain
For in the praises our God does reign.

On Satan's head Jesus will trod
Using the word as His rod.
Jesus never leaves nor will He forsake
Loud praises to Him you should make.

He's with us even through the fire
Let our praises to Him transpire
Jesus is closer than any friend
We are the victors in the end.

Never worry and never doubt
Jesus will surely bring you out.
Never rely on how you feel
There's nothing on earth Jesus can't heal.

When the clouds cover you
It seems you're going through
Just remember not to fear
The Lord Jesus is always here.

### Deuteronomy 31:6

"Be strong and courageous. Do not be afraid or terrified because of them, for the Lord your God goes with you; he will never leave you nor forsake you."

*Heart to Heart*

# Jesus Is the Answer

Daily distress
Causes a mess,
What should I do?
Call upon You.

I cannot shake
When I'm awake,
This feeling of gloom
Seek the upper room.

Problems do grow,
Bad seeds I sow
I have no depth
Through Him I'm kept.

Rising tide
Makes me hide
Where can I turn?
To Him I run.

Take yourself
Off the shelf
Put God first
For Him thirst.

Life will begin
You'll always win,
Stop all the strife,
Let God have your life.

### 2 Corinthians 6:2

"I tell you, now is the time of God's favor, now is the day of salvation."

*Heart to Heart*

# Jesus, You're Always the Same

Jesus, You are always the same
Jesus, so great is Your name
Loving, and giving and always living
Jesus, You are always the same.

Jesus, Your name has great power
Releasing in us hour by hour
Healing and cleansing, joy unending
Jesus, Your name has great power.

**Malachi 3:6**
"I the Lord do not change."

*Heart to Heart*

# Just Ask

Having troubles today?
You don't know the way?
Haven't got a clue
Of what you should do?
Just ask.

Things you touch
Don't seem like much?
Zigzag is the flow
As you daily go.

Just stop and ask.
God, what is my task?
You're doing something grand
Let me know Your plan.

*John 15:7*
   "If you remain in me and my words remain in you, ask whatever you wish and it will be given you."

*Heart to Heart*

# Letters from Heaven

Letters from heaven are inspirational sayings from the eternal point of view.

These letters are written to encourage everyone who has a loved one in heaven.

They are designed to inform those left behind of things that are happening in the heavenly realm, and to bring relief from any sorrow they may have because they can no longer communicate with their loved ones the way they used to. If those left behind accept Jesus as their Lord and Savior, they will see their loved ones again.

### 2 Thessalonians 2:16-17

"May our Lord Jesus Christ himself and God our Father, who loved us and by his grace gave us eternal encouragement and good hope, encourage your hearts and strengthen you in every good deed and word."

*Heart to Heart*

# Happy Thanksgiving from Your Family in Heaven

My first Thanksgiving up here this year
Things are glorious and full of cheer
I can't imagine not being here.
Loved ones once gone now all appear.

No more pain and no more sorrow
No more questions about tomorrow
No more hurricanes, tornados, or storms
I am relaxing and resting in Jesus' arms.

A mansion that is full, all my own
And daily praises around His throne.
I am so glad I have been set free
Happy Thanksgiving from eternity!!

***Revelation 21:4***
"He will wipe every tear from their eyes. There will be no more death or mourning or crying or pain, for the old order of things has passed away."

*Heart to Heart*

# Happy Thanksgiving from Your Father and Grandmother

Your father and grandmother want you to know
From heaven to you down on earth below,
We are sharing Thanksgiving together this year,
With praises and joy, all full of cheer.

We are not alone, there is the heavenly host
We are all praising God to the utmost
From us to you, we send your way
Joy and blessings for a happy Thanksgiving Day!!

With love,
Your father and grandmother

***Revelation 19:7***
"Let us rejoice and be glad and give him glory!"

# Happy Thanksgiving from Your Grandmother

Happy Thanksgiving from heaven this year
It's so exciting, I'm glad I'm here
So much joy and so much peace
Praises galore, they never cease.

No need for turkey or sweet potato pie
My mansion is full, here in the sky
Happy Thanksgiving, I'm not alone
Though you can't reach me by telephone

And we can no longer talk face to face
Love and blessings I send from my new place.

Happy Thanksgiving!!

With love,
Mom

*Revelation 19:7*
"Let us rejoice and be glad and give him glory!"

*Heart to Heart*

# Merry Christmas

From a heavenly perspective we send
Greetings from those who have been
Dear to us and now to heaven they have gone
No longer can we reach them by telephone.

In hopes that from your sorrow and your grief
This heavenly perspective will bring you relief.
So, Merry Christmas though I'm away
Be happy, share cheer on this Christmas Day!!

### John 3:16
"For God so loved the world that he gave his only begotten Son."

### Isaiah 61:3
"… to comfort all who mourn and provide for those who grieve… to bestow on them a crown of beauty instead of ashes, the oil of gladness instead of mourning, and a garment of praise instead of a spirit of despair."

*This is the end of the poems from heaven.*

*Heart to Heart*

# Praise Your Way Out

When the enemy has the upper hand
And those with truth will not stand
Life will seem very unfair
Things are caving in and no one seems to care.

In the natural it does appear
Satan's the victor, around here
But we know the end of the story
God prevails and receives all the glory.

Sacrifice of praise you give Him now
God inhabits them and Satan must bow
The two cannot walk together you see
From God's presence Satan must flee.

***Psalm 18:49***
"Therefore I will praise you among the nations,
O Lord; I will sing praises to your name."

*Heart to Heart*

# Thank You, Father

In sickness and in health
In lack and in wealth
We can all truly say
Thank You, Father, for each day.

Safely You keep us day and night
From unseen dangers and Satan's false light.
There is so much we don't understand
But we obey Your every command.

Thank You, Father, for all You do
For love and protection as we go through
For keeping us safe day by day
As we daily walk along life's way.

*Psalm 118:1*
"Give thanks to the Lord, for he is good."

*Heart to Heart*

# Thank You God, for Being God

Thank You, God, for loving us.
Thank You for everything, though we fuss.
I thank You for being God,
Even when You must use Your rod.

I know You do what's best for me
Even when I don't even see.
My faith and trust is all in You,
For only You know what I should do.

So if I need the chastening rod,
I willingly take it as I trod.
Through each and every day,
You so lovingly pass my way.

### Psalm 25:5

"Guide me in your truth and teach me for you are God my Savior and my hope is in you all day long."

*Heart to Heart*

# Word Portrait of Mom

By the road is where I stay.
People pass me day by day.
Weary travelers needing rest,
To them I gave my very best.

A bed to lay their weary head,
Grits, eggs, and bacon, to them I fed.
Some were strangers, some I knew.
Some were many. Others were few.

Dark or fair, fat or thin,
I didn't care. I let them in.
To be refreshed, to sit or eat,
Or just to chat and rest their feet.

My humble home has housed many.
Earthly wealth, I didn't have any.
What I had, I did gladly share.
I entertained angels unaware.

Men and women known world wide,
In my small home did abide.
Little did I know the Master's plan
Was to make me a friend to man.

Some achieved wealth and fame,
Others awards and much acclaim.
He gave me my own humble place
To show His love and minister grace.

Need to leave hustle and bustle behind?
Need some rest and peace of mind?
Need to be still and just sit a spell?
You are welcome to stop by Wardell's.

### *Proverbs 31:30b-31*

"A woman who fears the Lord is to be praised. Give her the reward she has earned and let her works bring her praise at the city gates."

# Chapter II: Encouragement

2 Thessalonians 2:16: *"May the Lord Jesus Christ himself and God our Father, encourage your hearts."*

*Heart to Heart*

# God Came

When the enemy caused us grief
And we thought there was no relief
In the middle of his wicked game
The all-powerful Savior came.

The evil one came with his offense
It seemed like there was no defense
Troubles rose up like a river
Our God came and us He did deliver.

The wicked caused our hearts to pound,
Even our lips quivered at their sound
Our bones and legs all did tremble
But You caused us to remember.

Though the enemy comes and we all scatter
You have complete control of the matter.
The evil plans the enemy tries to complete,
But our God will trample them under His feet.

Nothing happens in this day and hour
That You do not have in Your power
You have determined our enemies' fate
All we must do is patiently wait.

***Isaiah 41:10,12***
"So do not fear, for I am with you: do not be
dismayed, for I am your God. I will strengthen you: I

will uphold you with my righteous right hand. Those who wage war against you will be as nothing."

*Heart to Heart*

# God Does Supply

When you think you are without,
Count all your blessings and find out,
All your needs have been supplied,
And again, to you, Satan has lied.

Our Father in heaven knows everything,
He knows what to us, He must bring.
Don't fret, don't doubt, don't fear, or fuss,
God knows exactly what to give us.

When you are tempted to complain,
Remember, in all things God does reign.
He is the God of more than enough,
He takes joy in giving us stuff.

He gives to us above a measure,
By giving to us, God gets great pleasure.
If we really knew the real story,
God gives according to His riches in glory.

Don't let your mind take on this battle,
That what we want, to God, doesn't matter,
There is nothing more or nothing less,
That we desire, God will not bless.

*Matthew 7:7*
　　"Ask and it will be given; seek and you will find;
knock and the door will be opened to you."

*Heart to Heart*

# God Is Awesome and Great

Who can fathom such a great mind
That created the world and all mankind?
Whose thoughts are higher than we'll ever know
Who controls world systems and makes tech-
nology go.

So compassionate, loving, and always giving
Infinite, eternal, forever living
Gentle, kind, and ever showing His care
Daily leading us, as we walk here and there.

Who wouldn't serve a God like this
Who wants you to live in happiness and bliss?
Who controls and limits what you say and do
No matter what happens, He sees you through.

What an awesome God who rules and reigns
Through all our trials and all our pains
When troubles come, both small and large
We all know God is still in charge.

No one lives in a big glass bubble
In this life there will be trouble
It's through the suffering and the pain
We know with Him, someday we'll reign.

### Deuteronomy 10:17

"For the Lord your God is God of gods and Lord of lords, the great God, mighty and awesome."

### James 1:17

"Every good and perfect gift is from above, coming down from the Father of the heavenly lights..."

# God Is

Yesterday, today, You're always the same.
I AM that I AM is Your name.
Ever present You always will be
The beginning and end You do see.

There's nothing that will ever arise
That will ever take You by surprise.
Your eyes are constantly aware
You are always here and everywhere.

All authority and power are in You
There is absolutely nothing You can't do.
You are Alpha and Omega, beginning and end.
You are Almighty God, and our best friend.

Father God, full of love,
The Son sent from up above,
The Savior who came and died for man,
The Holy Spirit was part of the plan.

You are the creator of the earth.
You came to give us the second birth.
The mighty warrior and mighty King
Shalom is Your name. Great peace You bring.

You are the great shepherd of the sheep
You never slumber. You never sleep.
Your thoughts are so high and so deep.
You are the living Word. Our souls You keep.

### Revelation 1:8

"I am the Alpha and Omega," says the Lord God, "who is, and who was, and who is to come, the Almighty."

# God Is Here

When your struggles are hard
And your struggles are long
That's when our God
Will prove Himself strong.

Your trials keep coming
But you keep on humming
Though storms are raging
The louder you're praising

When you're trying your best
To pass all the tests
It seems as though
The problems just grow

When the tidal wave rises
With more life surprises
Where is my rest
In the midst of distress?

When you are weak
God is at His peak
Have no more fear
God is here, God is here.

**Psalm 46:1**
"God is our refuge and strength, an ever-present help in trouble."

*Heart to Heart*

# God's Love

We all seek to know
Why You love us so?
It's not because we're so kind,
Nor that You're on our minds.

Your love is so vast and wide
Us, you daily desire to guide.
You try to make us always winners
We fuss, complain, remaining big sinners.

Weary and tired You never grow.
Grace and love You always show.
How can we fathom love so great?
When all around there's so much hate.

Despicable hearts we have within
You still love us and call us friend.
You even died as the sacrificed seed.
Your kind of love we all need.

### 1 John 4:16b

"God is love. Whoever lives in love lives in God, and God in him."

*Heart to Heart*

# He's in Charge

Get ready, get set, and let's go!
Who's in charge of this earthly show?
The one who gave the second birth,
He's in charge of things on earth.

Through us the Father wants to stand,
He's chosen to use our human hands.
He has planned the very roles,
To keep and save our very souls.

Read His Word, stay in His face.
He will lead us to the place,
Of love, security, and grace.
It is promised to every race.

No time or season He doesn't know.
To Him no surprises life can show.
Be bold, be brave, and make a stand.
All things will obey God's command.

***Psalm 147:15***
   "He sends forth his commandment upon earth."

*Heart to Heart*

# Honor Your Father

In the home he is the king,
Order, security, and love he brings
Honor, respect is his just due,
Awesome reverence is his, too.

First to the Father up above
Who shows us daily His great love
Then to the father here below.
The one you live with and you know.

The one who knew you from your birth.
And is your covering here on earth.
Show him love without measure,
Do today, what gives him pleasure.

Encourage him in a special way,
Create a card with words you'd say,
Tell him how wonderful he is in your sight,
And that you appreciate him each day and night.

This is the time to take him to the store
Let him be the one who buys more and more.
Take him to dinner, give him a treat,
Let him order the things he likes to eat.

### *Ephesians 6:2-3*

"Honor your father and mother which is the first commandment with a promise that it may go well with you and that you may enjoy long life here on earth."

*Heart to Heart*

# I Love You, Lord

Lord, I love You with all my heart.
To others I will impart
All You tell me to do
For Lord, I really do love You.

Your sheep Lord, I will feed.
I will be whatever You need
For this is Your plan for me
Just to live and just to be.

***John 21:16***
"Yes, Lord, you know that I love you."

# I'll Fight for You

Obey what I say, obey what I say,
For this is My way, this is My way.
All I speak you will do,
I will come fight for you.
Simply obey and do all I say.

All your enemies will flee,
I am fighting for thee,
As you listen to My voice,
And make My will your choice.

You will not need a spear,
All your enemies will fear,
They will all turn their backs,
And there will be no more attacks.

Little by little out I will drive,
Until none of the enemy is alive.
You will never have a doubt,
All your foes I will put out.

All you have will increase,
Every sorrow will then cease,
All you do is just stand,
You will inherit all the land.

*Heart to Heart*

### 2 Chronicles 32:8

"With them is only the arm of flesh, but with us is the Lord our God to help us and to fight our battles."

*Heart to Heart*

# It's a Temp Job

We are on an adventure. We have just begun.
We're going somewhere. We're following the Son.
There are people out there, to us, who look like
messes
But to our heavenly Father, are future successes.

Serving God is line upon line,
Obeying Him, our hearts should pine.
Be very flexible, and easy to bend.
People are hurting, your help you're to lend.

This city you will turn around,
Satan's kingdom will fall to the ground.
Today, you are sent, yes, you I release
Go tell the Good News and help bring God's peace.

*Mark 16:15*
"Go into all the world and preach the good news
to all creation."

*Heart to Heart*

# New Beginnings

The old year is no longer here.
Sound the bells, and make it clear.
The slate is clean, the slate is white.
Let us start the new year right.

Renewed in thoughts, renewed in mind,
Unfruitful things all left behind.
Daily seek only God's best.
Submitting to Him and passing life's test.

Each day seek the Father's face.
Only He can show us mercy and grace.
His godly favor is better than wealth.
He prospers us and gives us good health.

Yes, the new year has begun.
We can make it a special one.
By seeking God and doing His will,
Our ordained purpose we will fulfill.

*Psalm 34:10b*
"Those who seek the Lord lack no good thing."

*Heart to Heart*

# New School, First Day

This is the first day of school
I will obey Your golden rule
I'll gain a friend by being one
The two of us will have some fun.

This is a place I've never been
When I'm upset I'll count to ten
It relieves the pressure and all my stress.
Now I can truly have good success.

I'm not good at trying new things
Fear and dread to me this brings.
This is a faith walk, I'm telling You
I'm depending on You, to bring me through.

These memories will be very dear
I'll always remember this first year
My first day in this new place
Lord, show me favor and give me grace.

I'm always trying to be strong
Hoping and praying nothing goes wrong
Lord, I need You close to me
Guiding me and showing me how to be.

### *Psalm 34:17*
"The righteous cry out and the Lord hears them;
he delivers them from all their troubles."

*Heart to Heart*

# Our Special Day

It is good to reflect
And to show due respect
To the one you love
Sent to you from heaven above.

To help make your life
Full of love and not strife.
Who help to make and not to break
Who help to give and not just to take.

One who is special in so many ways
One with whom you have had many days
Forty-eight years is quite a span
To spend with such a special man.

God purposed that this should be
He knew the special one for me
So, He formed you, the perfect meet
To help to make my life complete.

Together, on our special day,
Let's spend it in a very special way
Caring and sharing as couples do
Always remembering that I love you.

### Genesis 2:20, 22

"For Adam no suitable helper was found. The Lord God made a woman from the rib taken out of the man and he brought her to the man."

# Receive Your Reward

I fought a good fight.
I have won the prize.
I ran a good race.
My Lord said, "Arise."

"I've come for My beautiful bride
To be forever by My side.
On earth you did what you had to do.
You completed the tasks I had for you."

"No more sorrow, pain, or stress.
To Me you have been a great success.
In My arms you are gladly received.
Throughout your life, on Me you believed.

"Now you are free from trouble and strife
From Me you now have eternal life.
On earth your reward was never found.
You will now receive your heavenly crown.

"Glistening stones your crown will display
For every soul you won day by day.
You may ask, 'When, how, and where?'
It was when you showed others love and care.

"Come my bride, be with Me.
A mansion I have prepared for thee."

*Heart to Heart*

### 2 Timothy 4:7-8

"I have fought the good fight, I have finished the race, I have kept the faith. Now there is in store for me the crown of righteousness, which the Lord, the righteous judge will award to me."

*Heart to Heart*

# See Through His Eyes

Where were you when God found you?
All confused and going through
Drinking, cursing, and thought it was fun
Playing the lottery, leaving things undone.

Hanging out, dipping snuff
Doing all kinds of crazy stuff
God looked with loving eyes
Called your name to your surprise.

He caught your eye and showed you grace
In your heart He took His place
He had called you from your birth
To do His work here on earth.

Use His eyes as you look around
See as He sees, others will be found
Who normally look like hopeless messes
But through His eyes are future successes.

Lord, we pray that we will be
People of Yours who see as You see
Wherever we are, wherever we go
Through Your eyes, others to us You'll show.

### *1 Samuel 16:7b*

"The Lord does not look at the things man looks at. Man looks at the outward appearance, but the Lord looks at the heart."

# Shine Your Light

Keep shining your light
Darkness must take flight.
Use the Word on Satan head
Your steps each day he'll dread.

Brightly shine each day
As you go on life's way
Doing good, deed by deed
Sowing joy seed by seed.

It is then you will find
When thoughts of you come to mind
You have been Christ's face,
When you went from place to place.

***Matthew 5:16***

"Let your light so shine before men, that they will see your good deeds and praise your Father in heaven."

*Heart to Heart*

# The Father's Love

Us, He did form
And us, He'll transform.
With His loving hand,
We'll yield to His command.

Why form a people like us,
Who complain, argue, and fuss?
Who can fathom such love,
From the Father up above?

Will we ever, ever see?
That He wants a family,
Who will share His love and grace,
Who through them will show His face?

He is so patient and so kind.
Where on earth would we find
A father who loves and cares
And of our faults never despairs?

Oh, to trust and obey
Each word the Father will say.
This is the only sure way
To have a peaceful, blessed day.

### *Genesis 1:26-27*

Then God said, "Let us make man in our image, in our likeness." So God created man in his own image.

*Heart to Heart*

# We Win

When things do not go
The way they should flow
We usually say
"Not a good day."

When there are big messes,
And no great successes
We seldom do
Press our way through.

Most of us find
When we make up our mind
And begin to press in
Positive action brings good attraction
And then we soon win.

### 2 Corinthians 1:21-22

"Now it is God who makes both us and you stand firm in Christ. He anointed us, set his ownership on us, and put his Spirit in our hearts as deposit, guaranteeing what is to come."

*Heart to Heart*

# Your Light Is On

Your light brings lots of life
It frees others of their strife
For just a little while
Peace comes when you smile.

Shine all over the place
Evil you will erase
When you are around
Love and joy will abound.

Shine on Satan's spot
The light reveals his plot
All wickedness has gone
Because your light has shone.

### Matthew 5:16

"Let your light shine before men that they may see your good deeds and praise your Father in heaven."

*Heart to Heart*

# You've Got to Press Through

You're in the hustle and bustle of things,
There're all kinds of stuff the enemy brings.
Negative thoughts keep coming to you.
Say, "Jesus, Jesus," and you will press through.

When you're fighting the battles of sickness and
    pain,
The enemy keeps sending storminess and rain,
There's only one thing for you to do,
Shout, "Hallelujah!" and press your way through!

You feel you are on a roller coaster ride,
Moving so fast, you can barely hold on to the side,
That still small voice starts whispering to you,
"I'm with you, I'm with you, keep pressing
    through."

Confusion is everywhere it seems,
Darkness hovers and light shows no beam,
Put on your praise music as you used to do,
Get your dance on and press your way through!

Your spirit man is really crying out,
"Why do you keep trying," is the enemy's shout!
You have a mission here on earth you must do.
Sing and rejoice and press your way through!!

### Philippians 3:14

"Press on toward the goal to win the prize for which God has called me heavenward in Christ Jesus."

# Chapter III: Growth

Colossians 2:19: *"It grows as God causes it to grow."*

*Heart to Heart*

# Fertile Ground

Don't let your heart be stony
Don't let your behavior be phony
Let all your being be good ground
For it is there the Word will abound.

Let not your heart shallow be
So the Word can take root there, you see
It will easily be squeezed out and choked
When for the Word's sake you are provoked.

Let the Word your foundation build
Worldly lust and deceitfulness, kill
Cares of the world, cast these out
Growth will come without a doubt.

Beware and don't let Satan seduce
And cause you no fruit to produce
Be careful in all of your ways
Heed God's Word all your days.

Like the mustard seed so small
When it is sown, grows very tall
Like that seed, let of you be told
You produced thirty, sixty, and a hundred fold.

### *Colossians 3:16-17*
"Let the word of Christ dwell in you richly in all
wisdom… And whatsoever you do in word or deed,
do all to the glory of God."

*Heart to Heart*

# Growing Through Affirmation

It's good to have in this life
A little struggle and strife
When you've been through the fire
That's when growth will transpire.

When you've grown muscles before
And earned awards and degrees galore.
It feels good to hear said out loud,
"Son or daughter, of you I'm proud."

Accolades, accolades, let them come
It should not matter who they come from
You, the enemy wants to taunt
By saying, "I'm proud of you" came from an aunt.

Once it is said, and from the heart meant
It doesn't matter from whose mouth they were sent.
Being affirmed is a basic need
Our growth will excel by this one deed.

### *Isaiah 48:10*
"See, I have refined you, though not as silver: I have tested you in the furnace of affliction."

# Growth Through Affliction

In the midst of pain and sorrow
You don't have hope for tomorrow
There's a still small voice within
That says to you, "You win."

When there is grief upon grief
And you don't see relief
Deep down the pain won't cease,
He gives you His peace.

You know without any pain
There is no hope for gain
But this we all know
Through suffering we grow.

Knowledge is here. We still ask why?
Sometimes we simply must cry
Breathe heavily and sigh
When good people die.

We know that one day,
We will all go that way
No matter what you say
We didn't come here to stay.

**Isaiah 48:10**
"See, I have refined you, though not as silver; I have tested you in the furnace of affliction."

*Heart to Heart*

# Handling Adversity and Grief

When you have lost something or someone
Life's no fun and your shoulders weigh a ton
Speak the Word, on it you stand
Things turn around. You start to feel grand!!

Trouble's all around and there's no relief
Close ones die and you're suffering grief
The pain is so hard and down real deep,
You lie down, but you cannot go to sleep.

It doesn't help even when you realize
All these things happen and is no surprise
Just call on His name; that's all you can do
For there's no one else who can really help you.

Quote the Word and say His name
Changes will happen; they can't stay the same.
The Word will accomplish what it set out to do!!
Jesus' name brings supernatural power to you!!

These things do help us to grow,
Through all these things we know that we know
Jesus and the Word work hand in hand
On both of them we can forever stand.

### *Isaiah 45:19b; 49:13b*

"I, the Lord, speak the truth: I declare what is right."

"For the Lord comforts his people and will have compassion on his afflicted ones."

*Heart to Heart*

# Lose Your Mind

We serve a God mighty and great
All creation He has determined their fate
Nowhere will we ever find
Anyone with so great a mind

Why do we try to understand
His wisdom so awesome and so grand?
His thoughts are much higher than ours
We will never relate to His infinite powers.

"Lose your mind," to us He told.
"Trust and obey, My will I'll unfold.
Don't try to reason what I have to say
Acknowledge Me; I know the way.

"On your own understanding don't you lean
Have faith, trust in the things not seen
Your path I will always direct
Lose your mind on Me, obey and respect.

"So, my child, renew your mind
According to My Word, My will you'll find
You will live in peace with your mind at rest
Trust in Me for I know what is best."

### *Romans 12:2*

"Do not conform any longer to the pattern of this world, but be transformed by the renewing of your mind."

*Heart to Heart*

# Love Is

Sharing and caring,
Giving and forgiving,
Honest and just,
Selfless not selfish,
Adoring and endearing,
Not shaming not complaining,
Covering each other's faults,
Complimenting and exalting others,
Patient and kind,
Strength to each other,
Showing grace and mercy,
Not holding grudges,
Not taking revenge,
Not tearing down,
But building up.

### *Romans 12:9-10*

"Love must be sincere. Hate evil; cling to what is good. Be devoted to one another in brotherly love. Honor one another above yourselves."

*Heart to Heart*

# Valleys

When things don't quite go your way
Don't stop and wish for another day.
It's in these times we will know
Just how much more we need to grow.

Obstacles, they are our test
To help make us be our very best
To make strong muscles and give us power
So others we can help when they come to this hour.

*1 Corinthians 1:3-4*
"Comfort others as you have been comforted."

# Where Is the Child?

What happened to the child in you?
Did you lose him as older you grew?
The simple trust, the ready smile,
The spontaneous laugh you had as a child.

As you grew, childlike things you put away
Your childlike thoughts don't ever display
This does not mean put out the joy
That you had as a girl or boy.

The Bible says and I boldly quote
What Jesus said and the scribes wrote:
"To get into heaven like a child we must be"
Now that you are an adult, set your child free.

It's no longer vogue to wear a prune face.
So, wear a smile as you go from place to place.
Selfishness and meanness, get rid of these
Joyfulness, faith, and love display all, please.

The child in you wants to come out
To laugh, to play, and even shout.
Display your joy, and not your strife
Release your child, bring balance to your life.

*Matthew 18:3*

And he said: "I tell you the truth, unless you
change and become like little children, you will never
enter the kingdom of heaven."

# Chapter IV: Healing

Psalm 107:20: *"He sent forth his Word and healed them."*

*Heart to Heart*

# Pat on the Back

A pat on the back
give some praises
will steady your track
then your confidence raises.

Now and then give a pat
Encourage someone else like that.
It will brighten their day,
As they go on their way.

Pats boomerang and
Come back to you
To comfort and encourage
When you're
Going through.

*Acts 13:15*
"Brothers, if you have a message of encouragement for the people, please speak."

*Heart to Heart*

# Be Affirmed

You like to be number one in the place
Even though you don't know a single face
You are known by others far and wide
Yet, there is an emptiness down deep inside.

Keep on forging on and you'll become a success
Many accolades come, God you do bless
But when you turn and look everywhere,
None of your parents or loved ones are there.

You learn how to accept the hurts that life brings
And just laugh it off, it takes away the stings.
One day you meet a very special one
Who brings you much joy and loads of fun.

Your life becomes full of happiness and bliss,
no one else could make you feel like this.
He came and taught you just how to live,
how to love others and how to forgive.

Why? This lightens your burdens and lifts the load
Lots of forgiveness is needed to travel this road.
Offenses will come again and again
Forgive quickly, and have peace deep within.

***Psalm 130:4***
 "But with you there is forgiveness."

*Heart to Heart*

# Be Whole

God already has a healing plan
To bring good health to every human
Confess your faults to one another
This will bring healing to you and your brother.

*James 5:16*
"Therefore confess your sins to each other and pray for each other so that you may be healed."

*Heart to Heart*

# Free Through Praise

When the enemy has the upper hand
And those with truth will not stand
Things are caving in everywhere.
Life, right now, seems very unfair.

In the natural it does appear,
the victor, is the enemy around here.
But we know the end of the story,
God will prevail and get all the glory.

Sacrifices of praise we give up now.
The Savior inhabits them, the enemy must bow.
These two cannot walk together, you see,
From God's presence, the enemy must flee!

**2 Chronicles 5:13**
"They raised their voices in praise."

*Heart to Heart*

# Is It Fair?

Is it fair or is it not
to receive just results for what you got?
There is one who died for you,
Did He get His just due?

If we decide to be like Him,
what is fair will not be like them.
Suffering will come and so will offense,
Only His love will be our defense.

A debt He didn't owe, He paid the price,
Killed by others, that wasn't nice.
To be like Him we should desire to be,
The kind of Christ other people will see.

Things will seldom go our way,
That is a small price for us to pay,
Unjustness is all a part,
Of showing others Jesus' heart.

Is it fair? Don't go there,
You will see unjustness everywhere.
Don't let that noise throw you off track,
Keep serving God and don't look back.

### Philippians 1:29
"For it has been granted to you on behalf of Christ not only to believe on him, but also to suffer for him."

# It's Okay

When growing up, every child likes to see
Special loved ones in the audience be
But for you, there were none in the place
When you felt you needed a familiar face.

You came from a large family of ten
Attention, and affection sometimes were thin.
You learned how to shrug things off in this life
To suck things in when there's trouble and strife.

It doesn't hurt as bad, when you look around
And for you no family member can be found
You learn to be tough and keep pressing ahead
Even when you are in doubt, alone, and afraid.

Through good times and times that are bad
You learn not to be evil, and show that you're sad
For you, it became okay, if no loved ones were
    there
Applauding, and cheering in the audience's chair.

### 2 Corinthians 10:5
"We demolish arguments and every pretension that sets itself up against the knowledge of God, and we take captive every thought to make it obedient to Christ."

*Heart to Heart*

# Let Them Go

What is God saying to you?
What is He telling you to do?
Is He saying, "Let them go,
Those who hinder your holy flow?"

Maybe there're things in your life
That are causing you trouble and strife.
Ask the Lord. To you, He will show,
What's blocking your blessing; what to let go.

God is taking you to an unknown place
Unfamiliar ground, unfamiliar race
Not all are called to the place He'll show
You must relinquish your hold and let them go.

Another level God's taking you to
There's a greater work that you must do
Shake yourself, it's you God is sending
Let things fall off, on God you are depending.

Where God is taking you, you've never been
You don't know the way, on God depend
In His presence He wants you to stay
To hear His voice when He tells you the way.

*Hebrews 12:1*
"Let us throw off everything that hinders and the
sin that so easily entangles, and let us run with perse-
verance the race marked out for us."

# Lonely and Bound

Alone everywhere
But siblings many
Two parents there
You feel there aren't any.

Deliverance is nigh
You give a big sigh.
Even at the door
You say, "Never, no more."

There is a struggle inside
You try to abide
A stirring is going on
Yet, ideas are being born.

There's bondage down there
Hiding somewhere
Lord, search it out
So there is no doubt.

Turn on Your light
Make darkness take flight
In You I'm set free
You bring my liberty.

Thank You for freedom this day
Loneliness and bondage could not stay.
You alone the price did pay
I cried out to You. You took them away.

### Isaiah 61:1b

"He has sent me to bind up the brokenhearted, to proclaim freedom for the captives and release from darkness the prisoners."

*Heart to Heart*

# Radical Praise

I saw something. It was just a glance.
It reminded me of King David's and Miriam's
 dance.
Radical moving and their hands a-raising
Glorifying God with their radical praising.

My mind went back to a time in the past
When normal it was for praises to last
Twenty-four hours was nothing to do
In David's day, it was expected of you.

Seeing all this, brought joy to my heart
It got my attention so from it I didn't depart
What began as a glance became a stare
As I saw dancing and praising everywhere.

It made me sad as I thought about today
Most praises aren't done in this radical way.
More blessings are here than ever before
The dancing and praising should be even more.

I need to put me on a shelf
And completely lose all of myself
Perhaps that is what we all need to do
To allow radical dancing and praises through.

### *Psalm 150:3-5*
 "Praise him with the sounding of the trumpet,
praise him with the harp and lyre, praise him with

tambourine and dancing, praise him with the strings and flute, praise him with resounding cymbals."

*Heart to Heart*

# Set Me Free

Alone everywhere
But siblings many
Two parents there
You feel there aren't any.

You suffer abuse
You feel what's the use
Deliverance is nigh
You give a sigh

There's a struggle inside
While trying to abide
A stirring going on
While ideas are being born.

A bondage down there
Hiding somewhere
Lord, search it out
So there's no doubt.

Turn on the light
So darkness will take flight
In You I'm set free
You bring me liberty.

***Luke 4:18***

"He has sent me to proclaim freedom for the prisoners, and recovery of sight for the blind, to release the oppressed."

# Warfare Praise

Now is the time our voices to raise
As we offer to God our warfare praise
It's in the praise our God does reign
So, let us praise Him again and again.

Radically warring praises displaying
The enemy is fleeing while we are playing
Now is the time, all instruments use
To tear down strongholds and enemies confuse.

Judah in battle, is first to go out
Praising and dancing as they go about
Scattering the enemies without a doubt
Forcing through, praising the enemy out.

Stand up everyone the battle is on
Grab your instrument, blow your horn
Praising Him puts the enemy aflight
Warfare praises is how we will fight.

Radical praises are already back
God rules and reigns we all are on track
Confused, the enemy from us they must flee
Warfare praises brings our victory.

### Psalm 113:1-2

"Praise the Lord. Praise, O servants of the Lord, praise the name of the Lord. Let the name of the Lord be praised, both now and forevermore."

*Heart to Heart*

# What Happened?

There was a time this was the way
Fun and laughter went on all day.
Joy was always a part of you
Even in trials you were going through.

Wherever you were, there was no strife
In your presence there was always life
Others always wanted to be near
When they knew you would be here.

What happened as you grew and grew?
Where is that person we once knew,
Who brought so much joy
When you came around us as a boy?

Did someone steal your beautiful grin?
Are you hiding it deep down within?
What happened? What do you need
A kind thought or a kind deed?

To you, we sow both, they may help
To put back the pep you had in your step.
To lift you up, put away the frown
And bring back the joy and keep it around.

We want the old you to come back
And your old self to be on track.
The joy again with us you will share
And fun and laughter to be everywhere.

### Galatians 4:15

"What has happened to all your joy?"

*Heart to Heart*

# What to Do When You Feel Alone

Have you ever felt when in a crowd,
And everyone around was very loud,
That somehow they had all left,
And you are standing there all by yourself?

You feel your life is in disarray,
Your deep feelings you cannot display.
You don't want to talk on the telephone,
Nor visit others, yet, you feel so alone.

You are under a satanic attack,
He's trying to get you off the track.
You cannot hide things on a shelf,
Nor can you fight this by yourself.

You need to press beyond how you feel,
If you don't, you'll make yourself very ill.
Try praising God with all your might,
Put Satan's demons all to flight.

Someone you know who can pray through,
Call on them to help pray with you.
What you need is exponential prayer,
To scatter the enemy everywhere.

### *Psalm 68:6*
"God sets the lonely in families."

# Chapter V: Joy

Psalm 19:8: *"The precepts of the Lord are right, giving joy to the heart."*

# A Daughter Like You

I wanted a daughter just like you
Loving daughters are rare and few.
You were a special gift of love,
Sent to me from the Father above.

Today I want to let you know,
How proud I've been to see you grow
And love the Lord the way you do.
Daughter, I love you for being you.

May God's blessings come your way,
On this your special day.
May sunshine always brighten your way
Each and every day.

*Isaiah 9:6*
"For unto us a child is born."

*Heart to Heart*

# A Father's Daughter

She was always a bundle of joy.
With a silent language she'd employ.
Without a word she could always convince
Her dad to do anything. It didn't make sense.

Dad would come home at noon each day.
Her coat in hand, she would point the way.
Each day she knew and she would wait,
Her dad would come for their lunch date.

Sometimes she would change her mind,
And another route they would find.
By grunting and pointing another way
The route was changed that very day.

It's amazing what a daughter can do,
By grunting and pointing a finger or two.
She knows how to make a dad feel good
As only a daughter like you could.

She tells you how great you are,
And loves to ride beside you in the car.
She makes you feel you can do no wrong.
She builds you up and that makes you strong.

### Matthew 21:16b
"From the lips of children and infants you have
ordained praise."

# Happy Birthday, Son

Son, you are a son who is very dear
We are happy your birthday is here
In this life you've brought much joy
As a young man and as a boy.

You are our son, we say it out loud
A son of whom we are very proud
Gifted and talented, this we all know
You love to help others as through life you go.

On this day that's especially for you
Stop and enjoy it before it is through
As mom and dad we wish you the best
And hope this birthday tops all the rest.

HAPPY BIRTHDAY!!

*Malachi 4:6*
"He will turn the hearts of the fathers to their children."

# Our Daughter, the Ambassador

She always had a creative mind,
Anything built, she could always find.
To her brothers' sorrow, not joy
She would take apart each toy.

She could draw and paint for days and days,
Acting and drama, she always displayed.
She is a leader, this we all knew,
For wherever she was, there was a crew.

Every new family that came to stay,
In our neighborhood, she knew right away.
She always loved to meet and greet,
We were Janet's parents on every street.

She has always been on top of things,
Laughter and joy, she always brings.
God has given her the ability to "see,"
Not what is, but what could "be."

Our ambassador we called her then,
Through her creativity, souls she would win.
Before she was born God had this plan,
She would win souls, by being a friend to man.

Even now her life is not complete
Until Satan and his demons are under her feet.

Between evil and good she is making a wedge,
She is always on top, and on the cutting edge.

### Joel 2:28

"I will pour out my Spirit on all people. Your sons and daughters will prophesy..."

### 2 Corinthians 5:20

"We are therefore Christ's ambassadors, as though God were making his appeal through us... We implore you on Christ's behalf: Be reconciled to God."

# Sow Joy

Let us today, God's plan employ
And begin this day with His joy
Knowing happiness, joy, and bliss
Knowing God is doing this.

Christ supplies our every need
Do not let the enemy plant a seed
Of envy, jealousy, and doubt
To cause you to fret and pout

Don't murmur, complain, or fuss
Having a bad day is not for us.
We have come to set the pace
To spread love and joy all aver the place.

It's okay for happiness to show
To spread seeds of joy wherever you go
Christ wants to flow through you a while
Through your face and through your smile

These tasks have been given to us you see
Healing, restoration, setting others free
Showing others as we go our way
How they can have a joyful day.

Peace and contentment daily impart
Unity and love give from your heart.
Sharing joy wherever you can
Will make a difference to every man.

### Psalm 126:3

"The Lord has done great things for us, and we are filled with joy."

*Heart to Heart*

# Special Thoughts of You

You are a gift sent from God above,
You came to us all wrapped up in love.
You have from your birth,
Changed our lives here on earth.

Changed for the better I must say,
As we watched you grow day by day.
Inquisitive as a child but not very loud,
Today, a young woman who makes us proud.

To us you have been a great success,
And have filled our lives with much happiness.
So, on this your very special day,
As mom and dad, we gladly say,

May the best of everything come your way,
May God's blessings overtake you, every day,
But especially on your birthday.

Happy birthday!!

### Psalm 127:3
"Sons are a heritage from the Lord, children a reward from him."

*Heart to Heart*

# Tanya's Special Day

To us you are a beauty that's rare
Your gifts and talents none can compare
We want you to know we love you and care
When you need us, for you we'll be there.

If not in body, in spirit and heart
For in us you are always a part.
Your life with us was part of God's plan
You were the "chosen" to produce the fourth man.

So, on your own very special day
Celebrate it in a very special way
Pause and do something just for you
That special thing that makes joy flow through.

Happy birthday!!

*1 Peter 2:9*
    "But you are a chosen people, a royal priesthood,
a holy nation, a people belonging to
God."

# Chapter VI: Laughter

Psalm 126: *"Our mouths were filled with laughter."*

# Growing Old

Some bend over, others stands erect.
Some may stutter, others speak correct.
Some walk straight, some with a limp.
Growing old is not for a wimp.

You remember once you were tall.
Bone loss has now made you small.
Once you had 20-20 sight.
You could see clearly both day and night.

You once could eat everything you saw,
Fast food, junk food, even vegetables raw.
Your ears and memory were out of sight.
To do these today, takes all of your might.

You and your friend can barely hear,
He calls you dear and you're sure he said ear.
You go to the kitchen, you reach the door,
Suddenly you realize you don't know what for.

Now things get lost, especially your keys.
Look everywhere, even down on your knees,
Only to remember with a little frown,
They're in your pocket, you never put them down.

*Psalm 91:16*
"With long life will I satisfy him and show him my salvation."

*Heart to Heart*

# Growth

Through sorrow and pain
Strong muscles we gain
It's through trials you know
Where we must grow.

It seems such a strain
When life brings us more rain
But because of the shower
We bloom and we flower.

Comfort and ease
We like both of these
But we all know
They don't help us grow.

When times are real tough
And enough is enough
It is then we all know
To another level we grow.

*Isaiah 48:10*

"See, I have refined you, though not as silver: I have tested you in the furnace of affliction."

*Heart to Heart*

# Laughter

Laughter is easy as a kid
It's all around, never hid.
A large percent of childhood is fun
They laugh in the rain, and in the sun.

Laughter is good for you, too
Try it when you're going through
It's good medicine. Haven't you heard?
Look it up. It's in the Word.

Laughter is also a good exercise
Muscles relax and blood pressure subside
Laughter, like marrow, helps the blood
Cures diseases as through you it floods.

Youth returns, all wrinkles must flee
Laugh more often and you will see
Laughter calms everyone you're around
It lifts you up and releases the bound.

Don't wear your smile upside down
Put on a smile and get rid of the frown
Wherever you go, even in the hood
The universal language is understood.

Be happy; show joy as daily you go
Laugh heartily, let it just flow
Try it and see without a doubt
Your troubles and cares will all be cast out.

*Heart to Heart*

### Proverbs 17:22
"A cheerful heart is good medicine."

*Heart to Heart*

# Maturing

At yourself you must laugh a lot
As you say more and more, "I forgot."
This race is a long one, so have some fun.
Laugh for forgetting, maturing has begun.

You value each day that you are here.
Life itself becomes more precious and dear.
You stop to see the beauty in each sunrise.
You can even laugh at your larger size.

You can't be a wimp when older you grow.
What you once did fast, is now done slow.
Patience and laughter now mean a lot,
As more and more you must say, "I forgot."

*Psalm 91:15-16*

"He will call upon me, and I will answer him; I will be with him in trouble, I will deliver him and honor him. With long life will I satisfy him and show him my salvation."

# Our Sister, the Speller

When there was something she wanted you to
    know,
And your understanding with her, didn't flow,
"E-R-T-W!" she would yell.
"Don't you know? Can't you spell?"

Her brothers would come straight to me,
"Mom, what on earth could E-R-T-W be?"
There's no way to know can't you see?
She can't spell yet. She is only three!

Even then, she had her own little way,
To convince others of what she had to say.
Creativity was flowing then as well,
As she convinced others she knew how to spell.

### 2 Corinthians 4:2
"We renounce secret and shameful ways; we
do not use deception, nor do we distort the word of
God. By setting forth the truth plainly we commend
ourselves to every man's conscience in the sight of
God."

*Heart to Heart*

# Signs of Maturing

Here and there a little gray.
You simply wash it all away.
A little larger you begin to grow.
You buy a bigger size, so it won't show.

You wonder why others so softly speak?
Your hearing, you think, is at its peak.
More and more you ask, "What did you say?"
You don't realize your hearing is going away.

Once it was "cool" to work hard all day,
Then at night, dance the night away.
Energy galore you always had.
You were always upbeat, rarely ever sad.

All of a sudden you need more sleep.
The pep in your step is more like a creep.
Now you must watch everything you eat,
Salad, soup, and fruit for a treat.

Getting up and down has become a chore.
No running, or skipping, walking more and more.
There were signs all around, more than a score.
But all of them you chose to ignore.

Some would say you're as old as you feel.
Why do you think it's such a big deal?
Plan ahead and be well aware,
So, you won't say, "When did I get there?"

## Ecclesiastes 3:1

"There is a time for everything, and a season for every activity under heaven."

# Chapter VII: Peace

Micah 5:5: *"He will be their peace."*

2 Thessalonians 3:16: *"The Lord of peace himself gives you peace at all times and in every way."*

*Heart to Heart*

# Focus on Him

Very white, very clear,
We will start out this year.
No smears, no spots, not even a sin.
Refreshed and renewed, we will begin.

Only focused on His ways,
Doing and being what He says.
Everything will be just grand
Only on His Word will we stand.

*Jeremiah 33:3*
"Call on me, and I will answer you, and show you great and mighty things, which you knew not."

*Heart to Heart*

# The Promised Seed

Joseph and Mary
Were to carry
The babe, the seed
Earth's promised hope indeed.

So it was, and we did see,
The very place this would be,
The promised thing long foretold
A time, a place, it would all unfold.

Long they traveled from afar,
Not guided by any star,
Joseph, at first, was not on track,
To his hometown he had to go back.

For the Word God will move,
earth and heaven, His Word to prove.
In this case He used the government,
To send out a decree, so, back they went.

To Bethlehem, yes, Joseph's home
From which through time he did roam.
This was the time and the place,
Jesus was to first show His face.

Though it took a long, long flight,
To put them in place for that special night
So it was that the promise came,
The Savior, our Lord—Jesus, His name.

*Heart to Heart*

The couple came quietly and meek.
A clean, warm, dry, place they did seek
A place that had some nice firm beds,
To lay down their tired, weary heads.

A town with hustle and bustle all around,
Yet, for them no place could be found.
At the inn no room was there,
For the One who owns everywhere.

To the stable they were sent,
Tired and weary they gladly went.
The appointed time was already here.
It was the time for the babe to appear.

Though it took many years to be
The promised seed we did see.
Down from heaven to sin-sick earth
The blessed seed, the promised birth.

With animals all around to see,
The blessed, holy thing that was to be,
Quietly and silently they gathered around
The babe was born without a sound.

Out in the fields the angels bring,
News about this glorious thing,
To shepherds watching all their sheep,
They tell about this babe who's asleep.

In a lowly stable He lay,
The king from heaven born this day.

In swaddling clothes the angels told them
Go find Him and worship Him in Bethlehem.

Just as the angels did say,
They found the babe that very day
In a manger full of hay.
They worshipped Him, and went away.

Rejoicing and singing
Good news they were bringing,
Today, today, is our savior's birth,
Peace, goodwill, to all on the earth.

### *Luke 2:1-20*

Caesar Augustus issued a decree that a census should be taken of the entire Roman world. And everyone went to his own town to register. So Joseph also went up from the town of Nazareth in Galilee to Judea, to Bethlehem, the town of David, because he belonged to the house and line of David. He went there to register with Mary, who was pledged to be married to him and was expecting a child. While they were there, the time came for the baby to be born, and she gave birth to her firstborn son. She wrapped him in cloths and placed him in a manger, because there was no room in the inn. The shepherds were in the fields caring for their sheep and the angel of the Lord appeared to them and said, "Do not be afraid. I bring you good news of great joy that will be to all people. Today in the town of David a Savior has been born to you; He is Christ the Lord . . . You will find the baby wrapped in cloth lying in a manger."

*Heart to Heart*

# The Revealed Word

The word you read really stood out
It raised up off the page. What's that about?
It seems to apply to people you know.
Why this to you, God did show?

You see this fault in lots of others
Surely this word is meant for my brothers.
The speck in others God does see
Maybe He's dealing with that plank in me.

I don't want to be stiff-necked with a strong will,
Whose bad habits are very hard to kill.
Maybe like at the burning bush, I'll see
When I stand and listen, God is talking to me.

When the word from the page stands out
Stop and see what it's all about.
God at that moment to you will speak
Volumes of wisdom that will last all week.

There are things God wants me to know
To improve my walk as daily I go.
Maybe this is something to pray about
Or encourage someone else or clear up a doubt.

### Matthew 7:4-5
"How can you say to your brother, 'Let me take the speck out of your eye,' when all the time there is a plank in your own eye? First take the plank out

*Heart to Heart*

in your own eye, and then you will see clearly to remove the speck from your brother's eye."

*Heart to Heart*

# The Word

The Word is really the Father's Son
He was present before the world had begun.
In the beginning there were three,
The Father, the Spirit, and yes, there was Me.

As the Spirit hovered over the earth,
Things were void, creation had not seen birth.
No form, no life, nothing like this,
A formlessness; no happiness and bliss.

Until they said, "Let's make Us a man.
He'll be a part of Our eternal plan.
We'll have a family that will always grow,
Who will share Our love wherever they go.

"So, let us now prepare a place
Cozy and warm for our special race."
God spoke the Word and forth it came,
Everything needed and man gave it a name.

The Word, you see, is really Me
When man fell, I set him free.
A debt man owed and could not pay.
I came and paid it and washed it away.

*John 1:1-2*
"In the beginning was the Word and the Word
was with God and the Word was God. He was with
God in the beginning."

# Chapter VIII: Understanding

Colossians 2:2: *"Have the full riches of complete understanding."*

*Heart to Heart*

# A Moment in Time

Be about the Master's plan
That He has given each woman and man
Be about doing what God asks
For only you can fulfill your God-given task.

There are things that only you can do
They were especially assigned just to you
Don't you dare from them retreat
These things only you can complete.

God put in you His living Word
You must go tell it, it must be heard
You must do this; it's God's command
If you don't, the blood's on your hand.

God scooped out a moment in space
Called it time, for us, the human race
Life is short, precious, and dear
Live it for Christ while you're down here.

Your length of time here you don't know
When it is up you will surely go
You did not come to earth to stay
Time on it is only a breath away.

*Ecclesiastes 9:12*
"Moreover, no man knows when his hour will come."

*Heart to Heart*

# Are You Available?

He chose to use our human hand
So there would be a way to understand
A God so great with an awesome mind
Who wants to relate to all mankind.

His thoughts are so much higher than ours
He wants us to flow through His unlimited powers
God desires to use us so much
He wants to flow with our human touch.

Availability is all He needs
to produce on earth His great deeds
To do here and now, yes, today
what Jesus did as He walked this way.

Jesus wants you to say
God's commands you will obey
Living epistles would be every place
He would be living through your face.

*Joshua 1:7-8*
    "Be careful to obey all the law . . . do not turn from
it to the right or the left, that you may be successful
wherever you go."

*Heart to Heart*

# Are You Prepared to Receive?

Are you ready for what you ask?
Do you murmur over a God-given task?
Do you doubt or do you believe?
Now, are you prepared to receive?

If you believe when you pray
Your answer is on the way
We have an enemy you know
that tries to stop God's flow.

Don't look at the mess you see
Praise God for what is to be
Like Daniel, you must hold tight
For Michael has the enemy to fight.

Be encouraged, don't dismay
God has your answer on the way
Bless someone else while going through
See how quickly blessing comes back to you.

### Galatians 6:9
"Let us not be weary in doing good, for at the proper time we will reap a harvest if we do not give up."

*Heart to Heart*

# Being

The choices you make, you decide
Whatever they are, in them you abide.
Your being is what others see.
So choose the best you, to "be."

Life is full of many voices
Be careful which one guides your choices.
Bad ones are there to cloud your seeing.
Good ones are there to help your being.

Don't be too hasty. Don't be too fast.
Choices you make, may endure and last.
Be careful, choose wisely. Do it slow.
The effects on your future you don't know.

Watch what you say and where you go.
Watch how you act as you go to and fro.
You would be surprised both near and far
Others are watching to see just how you are.

### 2 Corinthians 5:20

"We are therefore Christ's ambassadors, as though God were making appeal through us."

# Best Use

Are you led by the Spirit of God?
Have you been under the chastening rod?
Have challenges been coming every day?
God has you on special display.

You may feel, "Lord, here I can't stay
I feel like just running away
This is so hard, is this really Your will?
If I stay here, me, Satan will kill.

"I feel I am not able to do this
I function better in comfort and bliss."
"Trust Me, My child, you will come through
It's in the brokenness I'll make best use of you."

*Psalm 51:17b*
 "A broken and contrite heart, O God, you will not despise."

*Heart to Heart*

# Birthing a Seed

Who was the one who gave birth,
To the Savior of the earth?
Who was the one who indeed,
Brought forth the precious, promised seed?

Who was the highly favored one,
God chose to birth His only Son?
Who was the blessed favored female,
Who brought forth the promised male?

One so young and yet so dear,
Brought our Lord and Savior here.
Though weary, tired, and burdened she came,
Carrying one favored above every name.

She had no choice of the place,
Where Jesus first would show His face.
Many prophets clearly heard God's voice,
And foretold His place of choice.

God, through the governor's hand,
Moved all on earth to obey His command.
One must go there, one could not flee.
For Bethlehem was the place to be.

Humans were used to bring about,
That which we no longer could do without.
For God had chosen to use mere man,
To help fulfill His ordained plan.

*Heart to Heart*

Today we enjoy and celebrate the birth,
of one who left heaven and came to earth.
To a sinful, ungodly, despicable place,
He did not punish us. He showed us grace.

Oh what mercy, kindness, and love,
That was sent to us from God above.
The present help that we all need,
Came in the form of the Father's seed.

There is a purposed time for a thing,
And in its fullness Christ will bring,
That which He has purposed to be birthed,
Will surely come to pass here on earth.

### Luke 2:1-14
The birth of Jesus.

### John 3:16
"God so loved the world that he gave his one and only Son, that whoever believes in him shall not perish but have eternal life."

*Heart to Heart*

# Check Your Fruit

Take this quiz, you may call it a test
See if your fruit is at its very best
Are you still stubborn and have a strong will?
Check yourself to see if you're Spirit filled.

Do others see you as humble, patient, and kind
when thoughts of you come to their mind?
Are rudeness, selfishness, and strife,
being seen coming out of your life?

Do you show kindness, gentleness, and care
as you go from here to there?
In your daily being, do others know
you are loyal and faithful as you go?

Do thoughts of you bring joy and peace
and troubles and anxieties begin to cease?
Are others seeing mercy, love, and grace
when they think of you or see your face?

You may not have thought of this before,
To pass you must have a perfect score.
In order for your fruit to be the best
You must answer "yes," to all of the test.

### Galatians 5:22-23
"But the fruit of the Spirit is love, joy, peace, patience, kindness, goodness, faithfulness, gentleness, and self-control."

*Heart to Heart*

# Disasters! Why?

Why do things happen as they do?
Disasters and trials overtake you.
You cry out for help but to no avail.
Everything you try seems to fail.

Everyone around is in the same tight place.
Wherever you turn you see a disturbed face.
You wonder, "Father God, are You out there?
Do You see what's happening? Do You care?

"We know You hate and detest all sin.
In ignorance we fail, and let Satan in.
What happened here You did allow
Yet, to your will, Satan must bow.

"I repent for my sins and plead for my brother.
Father, meet all their needs for we love one another.
You are the provider whether small or large.
No matter how things look, You are in charge."

### Hosea 6:1
"Come, let us return to the Lord: for he hath torn, and he will heal us; he hath smitten, and he will bind us up."

*Heart to Heart*

# Do You Hear Him?

God is always speaking to us
Quietly, softly, without a fuss
Telling us what we need to know
To successfully walk as we daily go.

He speaks plainly so we can hear
If we keep quiet and lend an ear
There is no toil and there is no labor
His words are spoken with human flavor.

Each person He does already know
What makes us tick and what makes us go
Sometimes He uses humor to explain
Our special path, our special lane.

He really wants us to understand
The plan He has for each woman and man
In us He always takes great pride
When constantly in His Word we abide.

He sees us through His loving eyes
Nothing we do takes Him by surprise
He knows each turn we will take
And made provision for any mistake.

### *Isaiah 45:19b*

"I the Lord speak righteousness, I declare things that are right."

*Heart to Heart*

# Fruit Inspector

God is checking your fruit out.
What are you like right after you shout?
When you are squeezed beyond your measure,
Are you sour or showing godly pleasure?

It is in the storm and in much pain
We grow in character so we can reign.
Does love and forgiveness from you depart
when you are serving with all your heart?

***Ephesians 4:32***
"Be kind to one another, tenderhearted, forgiving, one another, even as God for Christ's sake hath forgiven you."

*Heart to Heart*

# Get the Big Picture

The more you study, the more you know,
Enlarge your thinking, and make the mind grow.
A variety of things you should read,
Become more marketable in life, and succeed.

Gain lots of knowledge, broaden your view,
Others will come, seeking out you.
Prepare now, be well learned and well read,
Look out into the future, see what lies ahead.

There are some things burning deep within,
Ideas you see, that have never been.
The BIG picture to you is very clear,
You're holding it closely, to you it is dear.

Things are created and given birth,
Through ideas burning in people on earth.
Don't lose your passion, don't let it pass,
Patent your ideas and become world class.

### 2 Timothy 2:15

"Do your best to present yourself to God as one approved, a workman who does not need to be ashamed and who correctly handles the word of truth."

*Heart to Heart*

# Go with the Flow

Whatever way God's wind may blow
You always try to go with the flow.
Everything God's Spirit will know
You just learn to just flow.

He'll lead, He'll guide, He'll protect,
Flowing with Him gives due respect
Everything He says and does is true,
Only His best He'll give to you.

With His wind, learn to bend
You'll be the victor in the end.
He leads you with God's precious love
He only hears from God above.

On what He tells you, you can rely
Everything you need He will supply.
Learn to hear His still small voice
Heeding His will is your best choice.

He's the one who knows the way,
In His will you want to stay.
This is why you must always know
It's to your good to go with the flow.

### *Isaiah 48:17*
"I am the Lord your God, who teaches you what
is best for you, who directs you in the way you should
go."

*Heart to Heart*

# Know Your Assignment

Do you know what you are to do?
God created an assignment for you.
Are you aware you came to earth
With an appointed task to do from birth?

Only God knows your length of days.
He's given you ample to complete what He says.
You need to be about your special task.
If unknown to you, God you must ask.

It's not given for us all to preach.
But there are those only you can reach.
How can you reach them? Only God knows.
When you ask Him, His ways He shows.

You really should not hesitate
For your assignment you cannot wait.
There's an urgency; don't you miss.
Don't leave earth before you do this.

Salvation is great, you need it, 'tis true
So do others who must come in through you.
Pouring out yourself is the way you must live.
Ministering love is something you must give.

### 2 Corinthians 5:18, 20

"All this is from God, who reconciled us to himself through Christ and gave us the ministry of reconciliation. We are therefore Christ's ambassadors, as though God were making his appeal through us."

*Heart to Heart*

# Make It Clear!

Tell me now,
Tell me when
Don't you say,
"Just begin."

Order, a plan,
Is what I need.
Haphazard acts,
"No, indeed."

Tell me where,
Tell me how.
Don't just yell,
"Do it now!"

Structure for me,
Don't you know?
That's the way,
I best flow.

***Deuteronomy 12:32***
"See that you do all I command you; do not add to it or take away from it."

# Obey God

When the enemy hears what God wants you to do,
Immediately he sends his troops to buffet you.
They put stumbling blocks in your way,
To discourage you from doing what the Lord says.

We must ask God what we must do,
When the giants come up against you.
These directions only God can give,
He knows what it will take for us to live.

Giants in the land are nothing to Him,
He can easily get rid of all of them
When the Lord speaks we must obey,
we must do exactly what He says.

***Psalm 119:56***
"This has been my practice: I obey your precepts."

# Promised Success

God made you the head not the tail
Walking in His promises you will not fail
Good health and prosperity are a few of them
Obey His Word and only follow Him.

Trials may come and winds may blow
They are all needed to help us grow
It's in these times you know that you know
God's mercy, grace, and power to you He'll show.

### 1 Chronicles 26:5b

"As long as he sought the Lord, God gave him success."

*Heart to Heart*

# Teach Me O Lord

Teach me Your ways, O Lord,
Teach me to follow each day,
Teach me Your ways, O Lord,
To know just what to say.

Teach me Your ways, O Lord,
Teach me the way to go,
Teach me Your ways, O Lord,
Teach me so I will know.

Teach me to always know,
Your will to others show,
Teach me to always know,
The way You always go.

Let me be, O Lord,
What You want me to be,
Help me see, O Lord,
Like You always see.

Let me feel, O Lord,
What You always feel,
Let Your will, O Lord,
Always be my will.

### *Psalm 25:4-5*
Show me your ways, O Lord, teach your
paths, guide me in your truth and teach me for you

are God my Savior, and my hope is in you all day long.

*Heart to Heart*

# Understand Your Role

Parent, child, grandparent, friend
Just which role are you in?
Depending upon this fact,
Determines exactly how you should act.

Understanding one's role prevents abuse
Because you know your purpose and your use.
Moms and dads are instructors you see,
They model just how things should be.

Lots of love grandparents give out
Treat you nice and take you about.
Let you do many neat things,
Lots of wisdom to you they bring.

Children are God's gifts to man,
They are God's replenishment plan
Full of questions, always asking why?
Fearing nothing, anything they'll try.

Friends love and appreciate each other.
They will stick closer to you than a brother.
Friends like you even in your messes,
They cheer you on through your successes.

Your role you must understand,
So, you can take control over this land.
Dominion for us is God's command
Your role and ruling go hand in hand.

### Ephesians 5:17

"Therefore do not be foolish, but understand what the Lord's will is."

# Where Is God?

What is the matter?
My troubles won't scatter.
Everything is wrong.
Is God on His throne?

Never, never fear
God is always here.
Always seek His face.
Your cares He will erase.

God is always there.
He is everywhere.
Never, never doubt,
He will help you out.

### Psalm 55:22

"Cast your cares on the Lord and he will sustain you; he will never let the righteous fall."

# Why Christmas?

It's not the presents and the gifts
But love, peace, and joy that lifts,
That shows the world the true reason
Why Jesus Christ gave us this season.

All were lost, bound by sin here
When God sent His Son so dear,
To sacrifice and give His life
To rid the world of selfishness and strife.

Only Jesus could pay the debt we owe,
By allowing His shed blood to flow,
On the cross He paid an awesome price,
To rid us all from sins' wicked device.

Let's care, let's share, let's love and forgive,
Then we'll show the world how we should live,
For joy, peace, success is ours by choice,
It's ours when we heed His will, His ways, His
    voice.

### *John 3:16*

"For God so loved the world that he gave his one and only Son, that whoever believes in him shall not perish but shall have eternal life."

*Heart to Heart*

# Why Inspirational Poems?

Poems to help start your day
Poems to inspire you on your way
Poems that encourage your heart
Just stop and read them is your part.

You will find as you begin
More confidence and peace comes within
You will find everywhere you go
God's love through you will flow.

Stop, read, and inquire
So God's Word to you will inspire
Calmness, peace, joy, or a smile
That will comfort or encourage for a while.

Yes, poems can bring inner joy
One of God's weapons we all can deploy
Inner strength, joy can bring
Even through trials you can sing.

Why inspirational poems read?
They help you God's Word to heed
They help God's confidence in you abide
As within your heart His Word you hide.

We live a happy secure life
Free from anxiety and worldly strife
All because you stopped and stood still
And read a poem and discovered God's will.

### 2 Thessalonians 2:16-17

"May our Lord Jesus Christ himself and God our Father, who loved us and by his grace gave us eternal encouragement and good hope, encourage your hearts and strengthen you in every good deed and word."

# Yielded Vessel

Yes, Your will I will obey
Today, I'll do just what You say
I will willingly walk as You walk
I will willingly talk as You talk.

No more double minded I'll be
Yes, this is the real me
What I say, others will see
My walk and my talk will all agree.

The mask is off, I'm on task
I am doing just what You ask
I am doing what You say
Healing and delivering day by day.

People are being set free
And You're doing it through me
A vessel yielding to Your way
With Your help I will always stay.

Lord, I thank You, You're so good
Even when I'm not doing what I should
Help me to be just like You
And always do what You would do.

*Hebrews 13:18*
"Pray for us. We are sure that we have a clear conscience and desire to live honorably in every way."

*Heart to Heart*

# Your Journey

We are treasures in vessels of clay,
Fragile, delicate, handle with care.
Traveling daily through this life,
Filled with evil, trouble, and strife.

Don't dwell on any negative thing,
That each day seems to bring.
Positive thoughts keep on your mind,
It is there, your peace you will find.

When you are troubled, down for a while,
Encourage someone else with your lovely smile.
These things are all parts of running this race.
And will last until we leave this place.

The length of our journey we don't know,
Sow happiness, joy, and peace as you go,
Others who follow your steps will find
A path of love you have left behind.

Through storm clouds and rain
Through sorrow and pain
Our God does reign
And the sun shines again.

### *Romans 12:2*

"Do not conform any longer to the pattern of this world, but be transformed by the renewing of your

*Heart to Heart*

mind. Then you will be able to test and approve what God's will is his good, pleasing, and perfect will."

*Heart to Heart*

# Your Life Is Not Your Own

There are things you must do,
just because you are you
For you God had a plan
long before you became a human.

God sent His only Son
because He loved everyone.
Jesus freed us from strife
and gave us eternal life.

You too, have been sent
Just as Jesus came and went
You are called to be and do
things He did and went through.

When you hear the Master's voice
You do not have a choice
You must do what He says
All of your living days.

For you, Jesus has paid
His life, down He laid
Now that you are reborn
Your life is not your own.

### *1 Corinthians 6:19b-20*

"You are not your own; you were bought at a price. Therefore honor God with your body."

# Chapter IX: Why You Are Here

Luke 16:15: *"Go into all the world and preach the good news to all creation."*

Matthew 28:19-20: *"Go and make disciples of all nations, baptizing them in the name of the Father, Son and of the Holy Spirit, teaching them to obey everything I have commanded you."*

# Destiny

For every man
You have a plan
Only You know
The way one should go.

There is potential to be great
Within all beings You create
Little by little we are all driven
By the level of faith we are all given.

***Jeremiah 29:11***
"For I know the plans I have for you," declares the Lord, "plans to prosper you and not to harm you, plans to give you hope and a future."

*Heart to Heart*

# Go Get Your Land

Your trial is just a test
When you're squeezed, will you act your best?
Will you squirm and say, enough is enough?
Will you be kind when the going is tough?

The blessings are already ours
We wrestle against wicked spiritual powers
Before blessings come the devil makes it rough
Be very patient, strong, and tough.

The war is on against God's command
Like Joshua, you must fight for your land
You must be courageous and act very brave
Then fight the giants for the land God gave.

### *Joshua 1:1-7*

"Now then, you and all these people, get ready to cross the Jordan River into the land I am about to give them. I will give you every place where you set your feet. I will never leave you nor forsake you. No one will be able to stand up against you all the days of your life. Be strong and very courageous."

*Heart to Heart*

# God Has a Plan

For every man
God has a plan
Only you know
The way to go.

There's potential
To be great
Within all
You create.

Little by little
We are all driven
By the level of faith
To all you have given.

*Isaiah 48:15*
"I, even I, have spoken; yes, I called him . . . And he will succeed in his mission."

# God Has Need of You

God wants your life and all it entails,
He knows your thoughts. He reads all your mail.
In Him, He wants you to abide.
Let Him in. He'll walk by your side.

God will lead and guide you each day,
He alone knows the perfect way.
There are no secrets He does not know,
And there is no place He cannot go.

God decided to make you a part,
of sharing His love and His caring heart.
He created all, and made every plan.
Let Him use you. You "be" God's man.

### 2 Timothy 2:21
If a man cleanses himself from the latter, he will be an instrument for noble purposes, made holy, useful to the Master and prepared to do any good work.

*Heart to Heart*

# It Is Yours, Come and Get It

Don't let Satan break your bubble
You are the victor over trouble
Look at those things yet not seen.
Satan blows up a big smoke screen.

Your faith is what he wants to steal
He makes lies look like they are real.
Remember what is really true
Unseen things are real to you.

Promises to you God has made
Specific plans for you have been laid
Step up and just believe
Those things God has for you to receive.

He has great things laid up for you
You're the one to see them through.
No matter how great or small
You come and get them all.

Don't you ever, ever doubt
God will always work things out
Nothing can stop what God blesses
You are in for great successes.

***Jeremiah 29:11***

"I know the plans I have for you," declares the Lord, "plans to prosper you, and not to harm you, plans to give you hope and a future."

*Heart to Heart*

# Ministry

A servant is what we are called to be.
Helping others brings joy you see.
It's right in the center of God's will.
By showing love, you will be fulfilled.

We're to reconcile others with God,
As daily through each day we trod.
By showing others that we care,
We're entertaining angels unaware.

Everywhere we will go,
God's love through us should flow.
Being a minister is all our life's fate.
God made us servants so we'd all be great.

### Matthew 20:26, 28

"Whosoever wants to be great among you must be your servant. Just as the Son of Man did not come to be served, but to serve, and to give his life as a ransom for many."

# Naked and Unashamed

It is not good for man you see,
In this world alone to be,
Loneliness he could not take,
So, for him, a companion He did make.

While asleep God formed for man,
Of his bone and flesh He made woman,
For man by himself was incomplete,
So God made for him a help meet.

### Genesis 2:20b, 22

"But for Adam no suitable helper was found. So the Lord caused the man to fall into a deep sleep; he took one of the man's ribs and closed up the place with flesh. Then the Lord God made a woman from the rib he had taken from man, and he brought her to the man."

*Heart to Heart*

# New Things I Declare

Old things foretold did appear,
All former things once were here.
I AM that I AM, is My name,
New things today I do proclaim.

I tell you now so you will know,
Before they spring forth, I tell you so,
Old things have now passed away,
New things will start this very day.

For the time to come, who will hear?
Is it you who has the listening ear?
Who'll hear things that were never heard?
Those things declared by God's holy Word?

I do declare! I do declare!
New things come forth everywhere!
I AM that I AM, that is My name,
New things this day I do proclaim!

### *Isaiah 42:9*

"See the former things have taken place and new things I declare: before they spring into being I announce them to you."

*Heart to Heart*

# One Minute

He was born
Now he is gone
A precious minute that was all
One short minute he heard the call.

What can you do in one short minute?
It is gone before you are aware you're in it.
It doesn't matter how short or how fast
Your moment in time in this race will last.

Just make sure Jesus Christ you know
Before you check out and to eternity go.
Whether you live one minute or two
Salvation is what will carry you through.

### 2 Corinthians 6:2b
"I tell you, now is the time of God's favor, now
is the day of salvation."

*Heart to Heart*

# Purpose

You're on a journey. You're passing through
A path has been designed just for you
Your directions are given, you have a lane
Follow them carefully, they will not be a strain.

Your heavenly Father called you from birth
He has a mission for you here on earth.
A unique plan only you can do.
That's why you are now passing through.

Called out of darkness to His marvelous light
To always do and say what God says is right.
Showing God's love wherever you are sent.
Doing what Christ did as He came and went.

### *John 17:18*
"I have sent them into the world, even as I was sent into the world."

### *Jeremiah 1:7*
"You shall go to all I send you, what so ever I command you, you shall speak."

*Heart to Heart*

# Read the Book

To know Me, read the Book
Not with natural eyes do you look
If you use them you'll pass right by,
And never see Me with your natural eye.

The Book, the Word, are one you see,
Read it carefully and you'll see Me.
Faith to all I've given a measure,
Search the book for the hidden treasure.

Your spiritual eyes you must use,
To receive My Word and not be confused.
My Word is living and full of life
Keys to being free and living without strife.

As you read you'll see from above,
I came to earth to show you love.
My Father and I have so much love for you,
You'll see in the Book as you read it through.

The more you read, the closer I'll be
I'll draw close to you as you draw close to Me.
Take my Word and hide it in your heart,
And from you I will never depart.

### *James 4:8*
"Come near to God and he will come near to you."

*Heart to Heart*

# Run in Your Lane

Just as you run track,
no one runs back to back.
Each person has his special place,
In which he must run in this race.

God to each of us has given,
Purpose to which we are driven.
Only God knows the right way
We must trust Him and obey.

If you listen He will explain,
Exactly, to you, what's your lane.
To you and me He's given a measure,
Of faith to go find the treasure.

When you're doing what you were called to,
Fulfillment, joy, and pleasure will come to you.
God's purpose for you here on earth.
Was planned long before your birth.

The storms will come and so will the rain.
They are all a part of running in your lane.
But remember, each day the sun does rise,
So, complete your race and win your prize.

### Hebrews 12:1b
"Let us run with perseverance the race marked
out for us."

*Heart to Heart*

# Speak God's Word

God's Word has much power
Speak it each second, day, and hour
With mustard-seed faith you can say
"Uproot tree," and it must obey.

If you believe and have no doubt
Whatever you speak will come about
Mountains will move into the sea
If you believe and speak it to be.

You can speak to the waves and even the wind
Stop them, calm them, or another way send
You can even quiet the worst storm
So, speak to the elements, keep safe from harm.

You believe, so, you should speak
Utter your faith, even if it's weak
Faith the size of a mustard seed
Is all the faith you really need.

You are rewarded for what you say
Speak only pleasant words today
What you say can mean death or life
Speak wisdom and blessings not death and strife.

The mouth speaks what's in the heart
Let no careless words from you depart
God will judge every word you say
On that great judgment day.

*Heart to Heart*

Always speak what you should
So what happens will be good
Speak only God's command
Behind His Word He always stands.

### *John 15:7*

"If you remain in me and my words remain in you, ask whatever you wish and it will be given you."

*Heart to Heart*

# Submit!

Submit is what we've always heard
Submission is often a misused word.
It doesn't mean cowering or stuff like that
Nor does it mean to become one's doormat.

It doesn't mean others are greater than thou
For only to Jesus every knee will bow.
Jesus submitted to His Father's will
We honor God when His will we fulfill.

When our relationship with God is strong
Submitting to others doesn't seem wrong.
When we hear and do what God will say,
We have become willing His plan to obey.

God's Word is God's plan
For every woman and every man.
To every sister and every brother
We must submit to each other.

### *Ephesians 5:21*
"Submit to one another out of reverence for Christ."

*Heart to Heart*

# Suit Up

God's armor you must wear
To safely withstand Satan everywhere
Strategies and tricks Satan will try
Armor on? Back to him his darts will fly.

Don't you dare get out of bed,
Without your helmet on your head.
Wear your breastplate, it protects your heart
God's approval is the major part.

Always wear your gospel shoes
Telling others the Good News.
Proclaiming peace and truth as one goes
Available to God, as through you He flows.

Your shield of faith you will need
To ward off Satan's deadly deed
You can see Satan's sneaky attacks
Full armor on, prevents all setbacks.

God has already sent His only Son
Through Him your victory is already won
Your sword you must carry, there's no doubt
It is only God's Word that knocks Satan out!

### *Ephesians 6:11*

"Put on the full armor of God so that you can take
your stand against the devil's schemes."

*Heart to Heart*

# Surrender!

Don't box with God. You're no match.
Surrender now, be easy to catch.
Don't be like Jonah and run away.
Surrender to God this very day.

There's something God wants you to say,
To all the people He sends your way.
Don't be stiff-necked and harden your heart.
Yield to God, and freely do your part.

There is so much for you to do.
God wants to flow by using you.
Surrender now, don't toil and labor,
Let His words flow through your human flavor.

He chose to use the human hand
So there would be a way we'd understand,
A God so great, with an awesome mind,
Who wants to relate to all mankind.

### Mark 16:15

He said to them, "Go into all the world and preach
the good news to all creation."

# Task on Demand

Sometimes God will of you ask
A thing you think is an impossible task
In your mind you might say
"I can't do this, take it away."

But you know you must obey
Whatever God to you will say
You all surely do know
It's for your good, with God, to flow.

You have no choice
When you hear His voice
But to do what He demands
He wants to use your human hands.

All things He tells you to do
If you ask Him, He'll help you through
He is always there to assist
What He commands, don't you resist.

### *John 2:7-9*

Jesus said to the servants, "Fill the jars with water," so they filled them to the brim. Then he told them, "Now draw some out and take it to the master of the banquet."

*Heart to Heart*

# Tell Me God, What's My Plan?

Lord, I struggle just to know
The way that You want me to go.
Strong in this my faith is not,
Yet I know my purpose You've got.

Show me daily Lord, Your plan
For I want to do Your command.
This struggle within I give to You.
I receive Your peace for it is true.

I yearn to know Your way.
Give it to me day by day.
The path I alone must go,
So others Your love I can show.

I know You are the one
Who gave Your only begotten Son,
To bring to me all I need,
It all came from Your only seed.

The one who gave me His all,
Just because of Adam's fall.
So today I give all my strife,
To You who gave up all Your life.

You gave me everything I'll need,
That in this life I will succeed,

I send up this earnest plea,
Reveal O Lord, Your plan for me.

### Psalm 25:9

"He guides the humble in what is right and teaches them his way."

*Heart to Heart*

# The Battle Is On

There is a battle on right now.
Some wonder when, where, and how?
We must see with spiritual eyes
Become aware of Satan's disguise.

The battle is real we must all know
The enemy lurks wherever we go.
Seeking to steal, kill, and destroy
Unless the right weapons we deploy.

We must practice what we read
Prayer and the Word are things we need
It's in the battles we're made strong
Some are short but many are long.

Don't walk around unaware
Like in this world you have no care
There are no excuses for being less
Everything's given for your success.

Conquerors we are, battles we win
there is a battle deep down within.
Only by your personal choice
you win or lose if you don't obey His voice.

### Isaiah 8:9-10
"Raise the war cry you nations and be shattered.
Prepare for battle, and be shattered. Devise your

strategy, but it will be thwarted; propose your plan, but it will not stand, for God is with us."

# The Call

With a sound so quiet and small,
You must be still to hear His call.
Without a sudden, long, loud shout,
You'll hear and know He called you out.

When God calls, lend an ear,
Say, "Yes, God, I am here.
Show me what You'll have me do.
Give me strength to carry it through."

### 1 Samuel 3:10

The Lord came and stood there, calling as at the other times, "Samuel! Samuel!" Then Samuel said, "Speak, for your servant is listening."

*Heart to Heart*

# The Walk

Where I'm going I don't know
to us, the way, God will show.
He has the ordained plan
for every woman and every man.

It's by faith that I must go
Like the river I must flow.
God alone has set the track.
I must go forward and not look back.

Like Abraham, God will show the way.
What's left behind, He will repay.
Set your mind on His will to obey.
Begin right now, start today.

***Psalm 37:23***

"The steps of a good man are ordered by the Lord."

*Heart to Heart*

# The War Is On!

When the enemy comes in a disguise
let Jehovah God arise.
No snare or trap will ever matter
Jehovah God makes all things scatter.

Your weapon is God's holy Word
Faith is built whenever it is heard.
It's the sword used, not just read.
The weapon to use on the enemy's head.

Prepare yourself this present year
To conquer every given fear
Sent by the enemy to help destroy
To take our strength and steal our joy.

With a sound mind, joy, and power
Victory is ours hour by hour.
The key to our battle is agape love
Given to us from our Father above.

Through selfless giving Christ paid the price
That gave us victory over Satan's device
Let's all go forth no longer a sinner
Through ever battle come forth the winner!

### Ephesians 6:11
"Put on the whole armor of God so you can stand
against the devil's schemes."

# We Are Only Passing Through

Whatever we say or whatever we do
Remember, we're only passing through.
We will be humble and we will be just.
We will show mercy and we will trust.

Be gleeful, have fun, be full of joy.
Create good things; build, don't destroy.
Whatever we say and whatever we do,
Remember, we are only passing through.

Our God-given gifts don't compare.
Use them for others to show love and care.
God gave to us His very best.
That is why we are now blest.

We freely received, now we freely give.
There is no lack; now others can live.
God always knows what is best.
In this knowledge we can rest.

Do not put up any defense
If what He tells you doesn't make sense.
Just obey and it gladly do
Remember, you are only passing through.

*Heart to Heart*

### Deuteronomy 5:32-33

"Be careful to do what the Lord your God has commanded you; do not turn aside to the right or to the left. Walk in all the way that the Lord your God has commanded you, so that you may live and prosper and prolong your days in the land that you will possess."

# We Are Sent

We must go because we are sent
Being here on earth is no accident.
God has given us a Word
for others, that must be heard.

It is time for us to go
To those, to us, the Master will show
We pass by people every day
They all need what we have to say.

***Jeremiah 1:7***
"You shall go to all I send you, what so ever I command you, you shall speak."

*Heart to Heart*

# What's First?

First things first that's what we say,
As we begin to start our day
Make a list; do that please.
It's always best to set priorities.

When you're going by God's plan,
You cannot think like mere man.
Many times you may be quite tense,
What God said do, did not make sense.

You made your plans for today,
But God said, "No, go this way."
Hey, you don't have a choice,
You must obey the Lord's voice.

What God says is your command,
Do it now. Take a stand.
Don't be led by the majority,
God's demands take priority.

**Deuteronomy 12:32**
    "See that you do all I command you; do not add
to it or take away from it."

*Heart to Heart*

# What's For Me Today? Just Be!

What is the word for me today?
What to me will my Lord say?
Will it be something large or small?
Will it be anything at all?

I hear you saying just "be"
Is this really all You ask of me?
I ask You, Lord, to me show
I really do want to know.

To "be" does not seem like much
But as I go, many lives I do touch
I really do need to understand
This to "be," of me, You command.

It is you being what I need
Whether watering a plant or sowing a seed
It is you being the salt and the light
It is you showing love whatever the plight.

It is the right way you're showing
By living and experiencing as you're going
It's caring, sharing, and helping each other
So I will be seen as Savior, friend, and brother.

To "just be" appears like not a lot
But it puts you in a peculiar spot

*Heart to Heart*

You can't forsake and cannot sham
For just "being" shows others I am.

### Isaiah 41:20

"So people may see and know, may consider and understand, that the hand of the Lord has done this."

*Heart to Heart*

# What's My Part?

Help from us God does not need,
To plan our day or plant a seed.
Obedience is the appointed way.
All we must do is just obey.

Put Christ first, not yourself
Take the Lord off the shelf.
Don't complain and don't fuss.
The Lord is in charge, not us.

### Deuteronomy 8:1
"Be careful to follow every command I am giving you today."

# What's Your Lane?

Ask God, what is it He wants you to do.
That thing that can only happen through you
In your mind there is a battle.
Have you seriously considered the matter?

It would truly be a shame
If the Lord is calling your name
And you really don't have a clue
About what in this world you must do.

There is for us an ordained plan
God has purposed for every woman and man
Don't you think it's time to know?
The purposed way that you should go.

Pray to God. Seek His face.
He will show you the destined place
Where you should be, where you should go.
He will tell you all you need to know.

Ask God, why you should live.
What are people waiting for you to give?
God will make it clear. He'll make it plain.
So you can run in your destined lane.

What's your purpose? Why are you here?
Will you put it off another year?
Seek God's will. Plan for success.
Do what He says and you'll be blessed.

*Heart to Heart*

### Deuteronomy 8:1
"Be careful to follow every command I am giving you today."

Printed in the United States
200116BV00001B/148-1524/A